This book belongs to

_____

Grandma Will Always Dance With You

Story by Cynthia Smith
Illustrated by Ty Smith

Grandma Will Always Dance With You
Story copyright © 2017 by Cynthia Smith
Illustrations copyright © 2017 Ty Smith
All rights reserved. No part of this book may be reproduced in any form or by any electronic or mechanical means including information storage and retrieval systems without permission in writing from the author or publisher, except by a reviewer who may quote brief passages in a review.

Dedicated to my
Beautiful Grandchildren
and
My Talented Son

When your Mom told me she was going to have a baby...

We danced and danced, because we were so excited!

After you were born, Grandma was so lucky...

I got to take care of you when your Mom and Dad went on a date.

We twirled and twirled,
danced around and around,
and giggled and laughed.

Grandma Will Always Dance With You

We are such good dancers, you know...

So good, that even Buddie the dog wants to dance with us...

and the fish...

and the birds...

Happy Happy Happy!

Grandma Will Always Dance With You

When you got a little older,
you were always rockin'
and rollin' to music,
any kind of music.

So...

It's time to teach you a dance!

No way!

You are going to kindergarten?

So exciting, let's go!

Oh yes!

Then I remember ballet class, that was so much fun...

Oh my, you are so grown up!

Going to the prom, really?

Have you grown up that much?

You are so beautiful!

Oh my gosh, the time has come...

College graduation!

Weren't we just dancing to kindergarten?

And riding the big yellow bus?

Grandma is so proud of you!

You are so smart!

Grandma Will Always Dance With You

What a happy day this is...

You are getting married! Really?

Where has the time gone?

You are beautiful!

Grandma Will Always Dance With You

And one day,
beautiful girl,
you may have babies
of your own.

Grandma Will Always Dance With You

Just remember, no matter where I am...

I will watch you grow older, and...

Grandma Will Always Dance With You

Fun Finds

🌰 Find all the acorns

 Find all the birds

 Find all the squirrels

♪ Find all the notes

 Find all the flowers

 Find the fish

 Find the baby kitten

Made in the USA
Middletown, DE
01 May 2017